THE HYDROPONIC GARDEN SECRET

SECRET

HOW TO GROW MORE FOOD FASTER
— ALL YEAR LONG —

ALTERNATIVE
DAILY

CONTENTS

> "It used to be hydroponics was just a nod, nod, wink, wink, word for pot growing. Now it is accepted by consumers as a preferred method of growing high-quality food."

Michael R. Christian, Founder of American Hydroponics

INTRODUCTION

At one point in history family farms were the norm. People were growing food for their families and selling and trading with neighbors and locals. Today, the small farm is almost extinct, bullied by corporate giants and government agendas. We have lost easy access to fresh, local food. Sadly, this has contributed to the current health crisis our country is in. There are more sick and obese individuals than ever. Diabetes is skyrocketing, as are other lifestyle-related illnesses such as heart disease and cancer. We have food scares where millions of pounds of fresh, seemingly healthy food is recalled. People are hospitalized and some even die.

What has emerged is a food system that is massive and complicated. A system that includes centralized farms, large food processors and corrupt chemical companies pushing GMO agendas. It is estimated that just one percent of farms control over half of our food supply and that 60 percent of farm profits go to as few as 50 major companies.

So, what does all this mean for the consumer? Simply put, this means we can no longer be sure where our food is coming from and the food that we now consume is not as fresh as it once was, comes at a high price and contains fewer nutrients along with an increased risk of contamination.

Are we victims? Yes and no is the short answer. Although things have gone awry with our food supply, we can take charge. We can control what we eat and we can, all of us, grow an abundance of fresh, nutrient dense and safe food for ourselves and our family.

So, what is the answer? The answer is to go back to what our ancestors did, to grow our own food and support community gardens and small farms. The push is on as more and more people realize the state of our present food system and take matters into their own hands.

What if I told you that you can have a fresh harvest of nutritious vegetables all year long? You can even do this in a small space, indoors, on your balcony or in a simple greenhouse. You can be successful with little to no gardening experience. You can do this with hydroponics

Hydroponics is no longer a science experiment or futuristic objective. It is real, it is now and it is available to anyone who desires to grow fresh and nutritious food no matter where they live.

Hydroponics Not Just For Commercial Growers

Although commercial soilless gardens exist all over the world, hydroponic gardening is not just for large-scale operations. If you are interested in providing food for your family or even your entire neighborhood, hydroponics is a great option.

In this book, I trace the evolution of hydroponics through time and reveal just how easy it is to set up your own system in the backyard, on a patio, greenhouse or any small space in your home.

I reveal step-by-step instructions and tips for success so that you can have a bountiful harvest year-round, even if this is your first time gardening. Fun for the whole family, hydroponics is a great way to ensure that your food is safe, loaded with nutrients and delicious. Growing without soil is not only good for you and your family but also for the environment.

Now you too can have access to years of research, perfected growing techniques and the experience of people who have dedicated their whole lives to the pursuit of soilless gardening.

Are you ready to start your hydroponic journey? Let me be your guide. By the time you have finished this book I am confident that you will be, like me,

"Hooked on Hydroponics"

Susan Patterson, Master Gardener

WHAT PLANTS NEED

Plants, like people, need certain things to survive, mainly water, air, and nutrients. You notice that I didn't say, water, air, and soil. Yes, the soil does contain nutrients and nutrients can be added to soil but plants don't require soil per se to grow. Here is the breakdown of what nutrients plants do need to survive and thrive:

- **Nitrogen:** Nitrate is the form of nitrogen that plants use. It helps build strong foliage and gives plants their green color by helping with the production of chlorophyll.

- **Phosphorus:** Phosphorus helps with root and flower growth. It also helps to build plant stamina so that it can withstand stress from the environment, including harsh winters.

- **Potassium:** Potassium helps plants to grow strong and grow well, especially in the seedling stage. It also helps retain water and build plant resistance to insects and disease.

- **Magnesium:** Magnesium gives plants their lush green coloring.

- **Sulfur:** Sulfur help plants resist disease and gives a boost to seeds. It also assists in the production of amino acids, vitamins, proteins and enzymes.

- **Calcium:** Calcium helps to make cell walls strong so that they can resist disease. It is also necessary for metabolism and the uptake of nitrate.

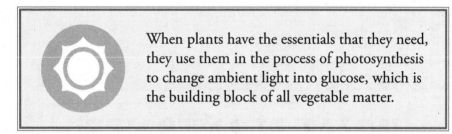

When plants have the essentials that they need, they use them in the process of photosynthesis to change ambient light into glucose, which is the building block of all vegetable matter.

Growing Plants Without Soil

Research has shown that plants do not need soil to grow and in fact, there are many benefits to soilless growing, also known as hydroponics. There are a variety of hydroponic gardening systems but they all have one thing in common: Plants are placed in a growing medium and nutrients are provided directly to the roots. When we grow plants in soil, they spend a great deal of energy growing a root system so that they can seek out the water and nutrients that they need to survive from within the soil.

FACT:
By providing constant and readily available nutrition, hydroponics allows plants to grow up to 50% faster than they do in soil.

Benefits of Growing Hydroponically

Control over nutrients: The nutrient balance in soil varies tremendously depending on what soil you use, organic, non-organic, enriched etc. With hydroponics, you can control the exact amount of each of the essential nutrients needed for plants to survive and thrive.

Can be grown in any indoor space: There is an incredible space saving benefit to hydroponics. Not only do you not need a massive garden space to have a soilless garden but you can even garden inside.

Saves water: Growing plants hydroponically uses two-thirds less water than conventional growing methods.

Affordable: Getting started with hydroponics is easy and won't break your bank. You can choose from any number of systems that range in price and many that can even be made at home.

Higher yields: Hydroponic gardens produce a great harvest and are extremely productive for their size.

Great for the beginner gardener: Growing a soilless garden is great for novice gardeners because it is very easy to be successful.

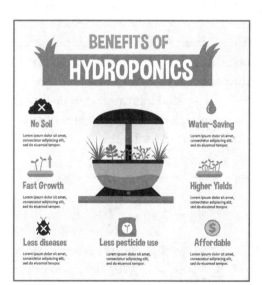

Year-round growing: When you grow a hydroponic garden it is not subject to the seasons. You can garden all year long.

Accessible: Because there is no back-breaking work involved in hydroponic gardening anyone can do it, no matter their physical restrictions.

No pesticides or herbicides: Hydroponic crops require no herbicides or pesticides that might contain toxic ingredients.

Good for the environment: Because soilless gardens use so much less water and space and no toxic chemicals, they are extremely environmentally friendly. Hydroponics also reduces carbon emissions because it cuts down on fossil fuels used to grow, store and transport produce.

Hydroponics is defined as the soilless growth of plants and was originally known as "water culture." The early days of growing plants without soil was embraced by out-of-the-box thinkers and tinkerers.

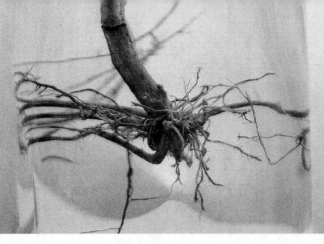

THE EARLY DAYS

You might come across writings that state that the planting methods used in the ancient *Hanging Gardens of Babylon* were hydroponic. However, modern research shows that these gardens were not actually hydroponic in nature, although the irrigation systems used to bring water to the crops was similar to the irrigation methods used in modern hydroponics systems.

Another often-mentioned comparison to modern hydroponics in the ancient world is the "floating gardens" that were built by the Aztecs in the 14th century AD. The Aztec population lived in the Valley of Mexico, which was basically a landlocked swamp with five lakes. They settled in this swampland and built their capital city on a tiny island in Lake Texcoco. To feed the population they built small islands (chinampas) made of soil, compost and sludge from the bottom of the lake. Although these crop islands were said to float, they actually did not float but were attached to the bottom of the lake using willow tree cuttings and other materials including stones, poles, vines, and ropes. There was no need for irrigation because water was wicked up from the lake. Because of the Aztec farmer's creative ways of composting and mulching, they were able to gather seven crops per year, which was enough to feed their entire population of 200,000. However, like the *Hanging Gardens of Babylon*, these gardens cannot be classified as truly hydroponic either. They were actually a combination of traditional, hydroponic and aquaponic systems.

Hydroponic Pioneers

Although it may be difficult to find ancient hydroponic systems, there is plenty of documented proof of experimentation dating back to the early 1600s. Let's explore some of these early pioneers who paved the way for soilless gardening.

Jan Baptist van Helmont

Flemish chemist van Helmont was actually detained in 1634 during the Spanish Inquisition for the so called "crime" of studying plants and other sciences, for which he was sentenced to two years in prison. Van Helmont was known for an experiment that he conducted on a willow tree to find where plants derive their mass, known as "the five-year tree experiment."

"But I have learned by this handicraft-operation that all Vegetables do immediately, and materially proceed out of the Element of water onely. For I took an Earthen vessel, in which I put 200 pounds of Earth that had been dried in a Furnace, which I moystened with Rainwater, and I implanted therein the Trunk or Stem of a Willow Tree, weighing five pounds; and at length, five years being finished, the Tree sprung from thence, did weigh 169 pounds, and about three ounces: But I moystened the Earthen Vessel with Rain-water, or distilled water (always when there was need) and it was large, and implanted into the Earth, and least the dust that flew about should be co-mingled with the Earth, I covered the lip or mouth of the Vessel with an Iron-Plate covered with Tin, and easily passable with many holes. I computed not the weight of the leaves that fell off in the four Autumnes. At length, I again dried the Earth of the Vessell, and there were found the same two hundred pounds, wanting about two ounces. Therefore 164 pounds of Wood, Barks, and Roots, arose out of water only."

Some historians have reported that this experiment was most likely spawned by Nicholas of Cusa's 1450 description in *De Staticus Experimentis* of an experiment he did not conduct. Further evidence of the experiment concept also dates back to Greek work between 200 and 400 A.D. While van Helmont's method lacked scientific grounding, his work and experimentation led to an understanding of photosynthesis.

John Woodward

John Woodward, another English scientist, tested growing spearmint hydroponically 1699. He grew the herb in a number of water solutions including rainwater, river water and water that was mixed with soil and then drained. The plants that grew faster and were healthier were those that grew in the solution that had been mixed with soil. This finding represents what we know today about hydroponics, that the minerals that remained in the solution gave the mint a tremendous nutritional boost.

Additional hydroponic research continued until 1804, when Nicolas-Théodore de Saussure concluded that plants were made up of chemical elements absorbed from water, soil, and air. A French chemist, Jean-Baptiste Boussingault, verified this proposition in 1851.

Jean-Baptiste Boussingault

French agricultural scientist and chemist Jean-Baptiste Boussingault conducted the first proper water culture experiments around 1840. Having established the very first agricultural experimentation station near Alsace, France four years earlier, this researcher made a number of important discoveries regarding soil chemistry and plant nutrition. He conducted a number of experiments raising plants in various soil substitutes including sand, charcoal and ground quartz, which he infused with a variety of solutions containing mineral nutrients.

Justus Freiherr von Liebig

Also in 1840, a fan of Boussingault's, German chemist Justus Freiherr von Liebig published *Die organische Chemie in ihrer Anwendung auf Agricultur und Physiologie (Organic Chemistry in its Application to Agriculture and Physiology)*. This work proclaimed that chemistry could drastically increase yields and slash the cost of growing food.

Liebig was the first to identify mineral nutrients necessary for plant growth. Gardeners know these familiar nutrients as nitrogen (N), phosphorus (P) and potassium (K). Because of this discovery, Liebig was known as "the father of fertilizer," even though he later declared that there was plenty of nitrogen in ammonia found in precipitation for plant growth. He was also known for his understanding of how individual nutrient components impacted crop growth, known as the Law of Minimum.

Ferdinand Gustav Julius von Sachs

In 1860, German botanist Ferdinand Gustav Julius von Sachs, the author of *Geschichte der Botanik (History of Botany)*, published his nutrient solution formula for "water culture," which was used as a standard tool for studying the nutritional needs of plants with only minor changes for 80 years.

Ludwig Wilhelm Knop

Knop was a German agricultural chemist who can truly be called the "father of water culture" for building the foundation of hydroponics as we know it today. Knop sprouted seeds in sand and fiber netting before transplanting into cork stoppers drilled with holes, securing them with cotton wadding and suspending them in glass containers filled with solution.

Following this, Knop realized that much of the weight of a plant can be attributed to the food supply stored in their seeds and that seeds provide nourishment to parts of the plant that form first.

At about this time it also was understood that plants needed nutrients in a soluble form and that there were far fewer soluble nutrients in soil compared to insoluble. This information helped to propel Knop's future experiments in water culture. Knop also concluded that nutrient-infused solutions that were too concentrated might do more harm than good, although he was not entirely sure why.

Although there were things that Knop was not sure of, he successfully grew plants without soil in 1860. These plants weighed more than their seeds and contained more nutrients. Knop's methods were used in 1868 by other researchers, who grew buckwheat in water culture that weighed 4,786 times more than its original seed, and oats weighing 2,359 times more. With these experiments, it was concretely established that healthy and nutritious plants can be grown successfully without soil via "water culture."

Building the Foundation and Putting Things in Motion

As successful as the culmination of research on hydroponics had been, progress in the area of soilless growing crept along during the late 19th century. The research that did take place was limited and focused on refining the necessary elements for soilless growth.

At the turn of the century, things began to change and inventions and discoveries, including the radio, the camera, the automobile, and moving pictures, became popular and research in water culture techniques gained momentum. Let's take a look at some of the notable contributions.

Contributors

1906: J.F. Breazeale's article *"Effect of Certain Solids Upon the Growth of Seedlings in Water Culture."*

1908: J.J. Skinner published the paper in Plant World called *"Water Culture Method for Experimenting with White Potatoes."*

1913: Conrad Hoffman from the University of Wisconsin published his research in the Botanical Gazette. In his studies he used paraffin blocks for growing seedlings in a liquid solution.

1914: W.E. Tottingham from the University of Wisconsin published in Physiological Researchers *"A quantitative chemical and physiological study of nutrient solutions for plant cultures,"* which outlines the importance of a balance of nutrients in the growing solution.

1915: John W. Shive published *"A Three-Salt Nutrient Solution For Plants."* In this publication, the author tested 84 different nutrient solutions and concluded that Tottingham's formula was superior to the four-salt nutrient solution that Knop had devised.

1918: B.E. Livingston and W.E. Tottingham published the joint paper *"A New Three-Salt Nutrient Solution for Plant Cultures."*

The True Birth of "Hydroponics"

A number of scientists were working with water culture and nutrient solution at the University of California at Berkeley station. Included in this group were Dennis Robert Hoagland, who began at the university in 1913 and later became Professor of Plant Nutrition from 1927 until he died in 1949. Although Hoagland's research was primarily soil-based, he also grew many plants using a nutrient solution formula that he developed and would later bear his name. He was careful to state that there was no such thing as a "best" solution and that it would require additional adjustments depending on the plant and the environment.

Nebraska-born associate plant physiologist William Frederick Gericke was also on staff at UC beginning in 1912. His research entitled "On the physiological balance in nutrient solutions for plant cultures" was published in the April 1922 issue of the *American Journal of Botany*. In October 1922, Gericke published a special article on "Water Culture Experimentation," which outlined his research growing wheat using a single salt solution versus a well-balanced nutrient solution.

The San Bernadino County Sun published an article in April 1928 called "Food Pills to Grow Plants in Water, Is Professor's Claim." In this article, Gericke noted that the gardeners in the future would be able to grow veggies and flowers in simple jars of water infused with "food pills," essentially cylindrical capsules containing combinations of seven essential plant nutrients.

More articles published in later April 1928 and distributed through the country. One stated on April 25th, 1928, "In announcing his discovery today, Gericke said flowers produced by the soilless method are sturdier, more delicately colored, and less subject to mildew than those grown under ordinary conditions." Headlines included "Grows Plants In Water: Chemicals Better Than Soil, Expert Says" and "Can Grow Plants Without Soil!"

Major stories followed in May and June, published in Alabama's *The Anniston Star* and *California's Santa Ana Register*, that took a deep dive into Gericke's research and highlighted growing plants without sun under artificial light. The same year Gericke, now on fire with soilless growing, announced that he would be showcasing his methods for raising plants in Europe with lectures in France, Sweden, England, Germany, Austria and Holland.

By 1929, the once-burning flame for Gericke's research had dimmed. It was not until an article entitled "Plant Pills Grow Bumper Crops" was published by H.H. Dunn in *Popular Science Monthly* that interest in soilless growing was once again fueled.

The very detailed article begins like this, "…through the use of a chemical "plant pill," administered to plants grown in shallow tanks of water, cereal and vegetable crops now are made to thrive under desert conditions of heat, arid soil, and lack of humidity."

The article points out that over 5,000 experiments under the direction of Gericke over the past five years had led to this discovery. The article notes experiment results such as asparagus stalks grown without soil and how the method increased the size of asparagus stalks by nearly 100%; potatoes increased in size by half; and the size of tomato plant yield can be increased by 40%. Further experiments on cotton, tobacco, wheat and cabbage showed similar results. In addition, cotton cultivated in water could be harvested sooner than conventionally grown cotton.

The article also discusses the potential benefits of soilless commercial farming and thoughts on using this method in areas of the world where conventional farming is difficult.

The article concludes with this statement from Dr. Gericke:

"… an area less than one-fourth that which, in my boyhood days, supplied the 'garden truck' for the family, will produce foodstuffs of variety, quality, quantity and value never dreamed of by the home gardener. Incidentally, the labor required will be only a small fraction of that needed for proper tilling of the soil. This, it seems to me, is the greatest value of the five years of experiments we have been conducting — that millions may be fed from water, on soils that hitherto have produced nothing but an occasional clump of cacti, or a few fig trees."

On June 27, 1933, Gericke obtained a U.S. patent for a "Fertilizing unit for growing plants in water." Following this, he set up his equipment in California greenhouses and arranged for research stations in other parts of the country to test applications.

Famous inventor Arthur Pillsbury, who was passionate about water culture and a photography expert, paid a visit to Dr. Gericke in early 1936. He took a number of professional photos of the amazing results Gericke had with hydroponics and also created a motion picture showing time-lapse photography of Gericke's work. With this new arsenal of promotional material, Gericke began conducting live demonstrations and speaking engagements where he incorporated Pillsbury's work. Once the press got hold of the images articles highlighting Gericke's work spread around the world and requests for more information flooded in.

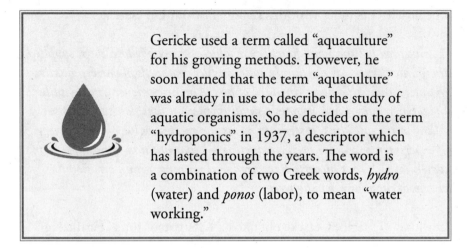

Gericke used a term called "aquaculture" for his growing methods. However, he soon learned that the term "aquaculture" was already in use to describe the study of aquatic organisms. So he decided on the term "hydroponics" in 1937, a descriptor which has lasted through the years. The word is a combination of two Greek words, *hydro* (water) and *ponos* (labor), to mean "water working."

Gericke was not quite ready to share his work with the public and really wanted to be sure that all aspects of cultivation were well-tested before he released specifics. He stressed that his work was incomplete when he spoke with his superiors at the university and that he needed more time to refine everything.

With more than 30,000 outside requests coming in from all around the world, university administrators felt it was necessary to release research results. Before doing so, however, they assigned Dennis Hoagland, a chemist and professor of plant nutrition and Daniel Arnon Jr., a lant physiologist, to review the work and create a report to verify Dr. Gericke's research and to outline the nutrient solution formulas and plans for equipment developed to date.

In 1938, Hoagland and Arnon published *"The Water Culture Method for Growing Plants without Soil."* Sadly, the paper missed many of the supporting benefits of hydroponics, which seemed to undermine the developing technology somewhat. Shortly after this report was published, Gericke terminated his relationship with the university but kept his research up at home. It should be noted that several experimental hydroponic projects were in place at the time that Gericke left the university.

Pan American World Airways

In 1934, Wake Island was chosen by Pan American World Airways as one of a number of stops en route to the Far East, a route that included Honolulu, Midway Island and Guam. Air service started in 1935 and, by the close of 1936, small hotels had been built on the islands to accommodate air clipper passengers and crew while planes are serviced after a 10- to 12-hour flight from one island to the next. Each of the hotels included a restaurant to feed hungry travelers.

The small system provided 120 square feet of growing area but produced a weekly yield of 30 pounds of tomatoes, 20 pounds of string beans, 40 pounds of sweet corn and 20 heads of lettuce. A similar system with similar yields was set up on the island of Iwo Jima, where crushed volcanic rock was used as the growing medium.

Entrepreneurs Embrace Soilless Growing

It was not long after Gericke's research that entrepreneurs came out of the woodwork looking to build a business and make some money. One such entrepreneur, Ernest W. Brundin, was a graduate of the University of California and a wealthy businessman who started his own independent greenhouse tomato farm. He experimented by himself, producing large commercial amounts of hydroponic tomatoes. Once he had the entire system set up he was producing 40 tons of tomatoes per year on one-half an acre. It was his thought that he would one day be able to produce 100 tons per acre.

Named the Chemical Culture Company, Brundin's business was so successful that by May 1938 he had contracts to supply eastbound and transcontinental passenger trains and steamships. He also sold his tomatoes on the other side of the country and in New York City.

First Home Garden Hydroponic System

Besides his commercial interest, Brundin can be accredited with patenting the first ever hobby hydroponic system in 1938, which he named "chemical agriculture system." In addition, he patented the first passive hydroculture pots for the home gardener. This double-decker system contained a nutrient solution below the growing pot and a wick that would carry the solution up into the plant roots along with a solution level indicator

Brundin was not the only person working with hydroponics systems. A former student of Dr. Greicke, Rolland Langley from Mountain View, California, started a 100-tank commercial hydroponicum called the California Packing Company. In addition, Langley was a pioneer in establishing hydroponics as a teaching tool in school. Thousands of teachers used Langley's small, leak-proof hydroponic kit that contained everything needed to grow hydroponically in a sunny window.

In August 1938, the Modern Gardening Sales Company of New York began placing ads in local newspapers for salesmen to act as distributors for hydroponic chemicals and equipment. George Zarafonctis, the host of the downtown Hilton Hotel in Lubbock, Texas, started a rooftop hydroponicum to supply fresh veggies for the restaurant. Many more such projects followed, proving the value of soilless gardening

Soilless Gardening Exhibits Abound

There was no shortage of exhibits for the public to learn more about this "new age/old age" way of gardening. During 1939, there were exhibitions at the State Fair of Texas and the San Francisco Golden Gate International Exposition, where glass-tank displays allowed viewers to see plants growing along with their root system.

New York World's Fair Exhibition

The New York World's Fair Exhibition was in the Heinz Dome at the 1939 and 1940 fair. The exhibit featured tomato plants being grown using "chemiculture," with plants rooted in sand and being fed nutrients through clear tubes. Although these were not the same tomatoes being used to produce the famous Heinz Ketchup, the company predicted that this would be a growing method of the future.

There was so much interest in the Heinz exhibit the first year that it was expanded the second year to include flowers and other vegetables.

Early Large Scale Applications

A 1938 *Time* magazine article featured a piece on the first commercial uses of hydroponics, piggybacking off of the UC Berkeley discoveries. Large amounts of mineralized water were used to grow crops of beans, tomatoes and other vegetables on a very small island called Wake Island in the Pacific Ocean. The island was a refueling stop for Pan-Am Airways and the hydroponic harvest was used to feed the airline's staff and crew.

After the lack of support from Berkeley, Dr. Gericke continued to pursue his passion for hydroponics. In 1940 he finished his book, *The Complete Guide To Soilless Gardening*. In his book he spoke of hydroponics of not yet being a precise science and that much experimentation was still needed but that there was much value in producing food on a large scale hydroponically.

When America entered World War ll in late 1941, Gericke was still pursuing and refining soilless growing techniques. In 1943, he put an announcement in the January 10th issue of the *Oakland Tribune* stating that he felt that he could best serve his country by sharing information regarding his agricultural "revolution'" and because of this, he opened his experimental gardens to the public as a learning resource.

Gericke further stated that "…his principal concern at present is that every backyard, however small or rocky, is converted to wartime production." For the next three months, every Sunday Gericke provided information on how the public could grow food hydroponically. Thousands of people visited his personal waterless gardens and many planted gardens for the war effort.

The Late 1940s and Beyond

The 1940s brought advances in soilless growing methods, including contributions by Robert B. and Alice P. Withrow, who were working at Purdue University. These researchers began using inert gravel as a rooting medium. They alternated between flooding and draining the gravel in a container so that plants received maximum amounts of both nutrient solution and air to the roots. This method was named the gravel method of hydroponics, or nutriculture.

Shipping fresh vegetables to soldiers overseas was a real problem during World War ll. It was at this time that the gravel method was given its first real time large-scale test by the U.S. Armed Forces. In 1945 the U.S. Air Force began to provide its personnel with fresh veggies by practicing hydroponics on a big scale, breathing new life into soilless gardening.

A large hydroponic farm was built on Ascension Island in the South Atlantic. This island was used as fuel stop for the United States Air Force and was completely barren. Plants were grown in a gravel medium with a nutrient solution pumped into the gravel.

 Can you image a garden system the size of your bedroom producing so much food? You could feed your family and your entire neighborhood with this!

The U.S. Army and the Royal British Air Force employed soilless gardening to provide fresh food to service men and women. Millions of tons of vegetables were produced during the war. After the war the military command continued to use hydroponics. The U.S. Army has a hydroponics branch, which grew more than 8 million lbs of fresh produce in 1952.

The world's largest post wartime hydroponic installation, one covering 55 acres, was established in Chofu, Japan. Conventional farming was not an option in Japan because of the practice of using "night soil," which contained human excreta as a fertilizer. Because of this, the soil was highly contaminated with bacteria that the Japanese were immune to but the troops were not. This water culture garden was in operation for more than 15 years.

Commercial Gardens

After the war, a number of commercial systems were set up, mostly in Florida. Although many of these systems were poorly constructed the commercial use of hydroponics flourished around the world in countries, including in Italy, Spain, France, England, Germany, Sweden, the USSR and Israel. Although there were plenty of kinks to be worked out in the systems, the interest in water culture grew mostly because no soil was needed and a large harvest could come from a very small system. In addition, when managed properly, the quality of the vegetables was superior and had a longer shelf life than conventionally grown vegetables.

Oil and mining companies also hopped on the hydroponic train and created large gardens at some to their installations around the globe where conventional farming methods were not feasible.

Feeding the World Hydroponically

Hydroponic gardens exist today that feed millions of people. Systems flourish in the dry and isolated desert regions of Israel, Lebanon and Kuwait, and on the island of Ceylon and the Philippines. Rooftops in Calcutta and in dusty villages of West Bengal use hydroponic growing methods to produce a harvest where conventional methods have failed to yield.

Just about every state in America has a thriving hydroponic greenhouse industry. Canada uses soilless growing methods and one half of Vancouver Island's tomato crops are hydroponically grown. There are even hydroponic systems set up in American nuclear submarines, Russian space stations and offshore drilling rigs. Zoos use hydroponics to keep animals healthy and race horses are fed grass that is grown hydroponically year round. Soilless growing reaches as far north as Baffin Island and Eskimo Point in the Canadian Arctic.

Growing food without soil has solved many of the world's hunger problems and made fresh food available in places where it was previously not possible.

UNDERSTANDING THE HYDROPONIC SYSTEM

The fun thing about hydroponics is that there are a number of different types of systems available for growing and some can even be combined for a super system. Each of these systems can be used to create a sustainable garden for growing food.

 Recent surveys have indicated that more than 1 million household soilless culture units operate in the United States for the production of food alone.

Key Elements of a Hydroponic System

Hydroponic systems can vary, but they all have similar components.

Grow Lights

If you grow plants indoors you must provide some form of light for optimal growth. Natural daylight is best. If you have a bright sunny window you might just be able to grow without any supplemental light. When growing vegetables outdoors, plants require between 4 and 8 hours of direct sunlight and a total of at least 10 hours of bright light - the combination of direct and indirect sun. If you are north of the equator, you will need a south-facing window for winter growing.

With a grow light you can be successful no matter where you place your garden. Using a grow light takes the guessing game out of making sure your plants are getting enough light. The best case scenario for hydroponic plants is a sunny window supplemented with a grow light.

Choosing the best light can be a bit challenging but don't dismay. There are lots of options, depending on the size of your system and what you are growing. When growing hydroponically, the main objective is to imitate this outdoor light. Plan to provide at least 14 and up to 16 hours of bright artificial light followed by darkness to complete each 24 hour day cycle. Keep in mind that the darkness is just as vital as the light. Just like animals, plants need time to rest and metabolize.

The best lights for home hydroponic growing include:

- **54 Watt High Output Fluorescent T5** - Fluorescent lighting is fine for lettuces, leafy greens and most herbs. The work really well for starting seedlings and cuttings and are the least expensive lights you can buy for hydroponic growing. They are also nice and cool. The downside of these lights is that they don't have the right spectrum needed for fruiting vegetables and flowering plants. If you are just going to grow leafy veggies, lettuces, spinach, chard, herbs, etc. this type of light works fine. For best results, keep the lights 4 inches to 6 inches above plants. Don't worry, these are cool lights that won't burn the plants. Use 40 watts per square foot of gardening space.

- **H.I.D. (High Intensity Discharge)** - These lights put out quite a bit of heat but they are the best lamps available for indoor hydroponics gardens. You can grow any leafing, flowering or fruiting crops under these lights because they provide the right spectrum needed and are very close to what the sun provides. There are two types of bulbs available, MH (metal halide) and HPS (high pressure sodium). The MH is a very good all-around light and is fine for most veggies. If your budget only allows for one bulb, get a metal halide one. You can generally find a good 400 watt MH lamp with a bulb for about $140. The HPS bulb is best for the flowering/fruiting stage of vegetables but is not entirely necessary. If you can afford to purchase a conversion lamp that takes both bulbs that is great. Use the MH for the vegetative growing stage and switch to the HPS when the flowers appear. You can generally find a good conversion lamp including both bulbs for about $200.

- **LED Grow Lights** - LED stands for light-emitting diode. The nice thing about these bulbs is that they use about half of the electricity of traditional lighting, the bulbs last for a very long time and they provide cool lighting. It is important not to purchase super cheap LED lights that make big promises. You really do get what you pay for. A good mid-range system will cost between $350 and $500 and this is a good place to start. Keep in mind, LED's will cost most upfront but offer energy savings in the long run.

Growing Mediums

Basically a growing medium is what replaces the soil in natural cultivation. There are a number of different types of mediums to choose from depending on what growing system you choose. The growing mediums hold all the nutrients that you need for growth

- **Rockwool** - Rockwool blocks are useful for starting seedlings and in many systems you don't have to remove the seedlings from the blocks. You can simply transfer the entire block to your grow pot. Because rockwool is naturally high in pH it is necessary to soak them before use. Rockwool is a great option for a drip system but watch that it does not become oversaturated.

- **Coco Coir** - Made from the husks of coconuts, this medium is popular in soilless growing. Coconut husks protect coconuts from damage from the sun, sea and the air and offer the same protective elements to plants. On the upside, it also looks a lot like soil but can hold up to ten times its weight in water. Coco coir works well when mixed 50/50 with perlite as the coco coir retains nutrients while the perlite retains oxygen. Be sure to choose a nutrient solution specifically made for this medium.

- **Expanded Clay Pellets** - As their name suggest, these pellets expand when placed in water to form porous balls. They hold seedling in place while still providing roots access to oxygen and water. Clay pellets are heavy and you can quickly have a weight issue if you use a lot of them. Also, they are prone to drying out if you use a lot of them. This medium is perfect for a drip system.

- **Perlite** - Perlite is volcanic rock that is very light and porous. This material is often used in conventional gardening to help retain oxygen levels. Because of its light weight, perlite is easily washed away or shifted to another location. Because of this, it is often mixed with another medium such as coco coir or vermiculite.

- **Vermiculite** - Vermiculite is a mineral that transforms to pebbles when it is heated. It holds water and pulls nutrients upwards well making it a great option for hydroponic gardening. One drawback is that it can actually hold too much water and it can be a little pricey.The best way to use vermiculite is to use it as part of a blend, using a small amount mixed with other mediums.

- **Gravel** - If you are on a tight budget, gravel is the best option. It must be washed before it is used to remove bacteria that could harm plant roots. It is also quite heavy so be sure that your system has the structural integrity to withstand the weight.

 Note: Peat moss, which is commonly used in hydroponic gardening, is not included in the above medium list as it is not a renewable resource.

Nutrient Solution

All plants need nutrients in order to live. In the natural world, plants get their nutrients for the soil and additives such as compost, manure etc. Plants grown in hydroponic gardens are not grown in soil, so the nutrients must be delivered directed through the watering solution.

Nutrients are divided into two groups: macronutrients and micronutrients. Macronutrients are those that plants need in large quantities and include carbon, phosphorous, hydrogen, nitrogen, oxygen, sulfur, potassium, magnesium and calcium. Micronutrients are only needed in small amounts although they are essential. Micronutrients include zinc, nickel, boron, copper, iron, manganese, molybdenum, boron and chlorine.

If a plant does not have these elements it can't build molecules, undergo enzymatic reactions and complete its life cycle. What this boils down to is that hydroponic gardeners will not see fruit or veggies on their plants without the proper nutrients.

You can purchase pre-made nutrient solution or make your own. The easiest is to purchase a pre-mixed liquid or powder that is added to water. Follow the directions carefully for mixing the concentrate.

pH: After mixing the solution, let it set for a few minutes to settle. Check the pH and adjust as needed. It is much easier to start off with the correct pH as that is easier to maintain.

Different plants prefer different pH balances. It is important to note that plants won't be able to absorb the nutrients that they need if the pH is too high or too low. After you have added the nutrients, measure the pH using a litmus test strip, liquid test kit or an electronic testing pen. A good baseline pH is to keep it between 5.5 and 6.5. If you need to make changes to the acidity you can raise it by adding phosphoric acid and lower it by adding lemon juice. You can also purchase hydroponic products that will adjust the acidity.

Other Additives

There are a number of different additives that you can add to your system depending on desired results. Although these nutrients are not necessary some people like to use them for enhanced results. Just be sure to do your research before adding anything.

- **Bloom maximizers** - These additives increase size and bloom are high in phosphorus and potassium. Bloom maximizers are used only during the flowering stage of growth and must be monitored so as not to cause nutrient burn.

- **Mycorrhizae and other fungi** - Mycorrhizae are small fungal filaments that penetrate the roots and increase their surface area. In addition, they gather and break down certain nutrients. Mycorrhizae exist in nature with almost all plant species and help them take up nutrients and water and, in return, they get sugar from the plant photosynthesis process. Mycorrhizal fungi can be added directly to the nutrient solution.

- **Vitamins and enzymes** - Thiamine (vitamin B-1) helps to support and strengthen plant immune systems and roots, which helps them to withstand stress and disease. Enzymes help plants take up nutrients by breaking them down while preventing algae growth.

- **Root stimulators** - Soil contains both harmful and beneficial microbes that can help or hinder plant growth. Root stimulators are compounds that bring healthy mircrobes, like those in the soil, to your hydroponics system. They build plants immune systems, increase access to nitrogen, and help develop a strong root system faster. It is best to add root stimulators at the beginning of the growth cycle and they will reproduce throughout the plant's life cycle.

 Do your homework before purchasing any nutrients. Read product reviews and talk to other hydroponic growers before choosing the best product for your needs.

Water

We so often take water for granted. Good, clean water is essential for successful hydroponic growing. The best choice is distilled or reverse osmosis water. Tap water can have pollutants and additives in it and should be avoided.

Nutrient Reservoir

Nutrient reservoirs are the containers that hold the nutrient solution and water in a hydroponic system. The best nutrient reservoirs are made from heavy-duty plastic with some type of UV protection. The important thing with choosing a reservoir is to get one big enough and be sure that it is food-grade plastic so that nothing poisonous leeches into the nutrient solution and water supply. Follow these general rules to determine the size that you need:

- **Small plants** - Supply a minimum of ½ gallon of water per plant
- **Medium plants** - Supply 1½ gallons of water per plant
- **Large plants** - Supply 2½ gallons of water per plant

Grow Tray

The grow tray holds the plants and keeps them separated from the nutrient solution. Also known as grow chambers, pots will vary depending on the type of system you use.

Pump

The purpose of the pump in the hydroponic system is to oxygenate the water and prevent algae from growing in the reservoir. This functions in a similar way to an aquarium. The circulation makes it easier to ensure fresh and clean water. It is important to understand pump specifications that indicate how high they will pump. This is measured in HEAD. If a pump is rated at 3 feet of HEAD, then it will pump 3 feet to the top of the inlet. If the pump only has a PSI (pounds per square inch) rating, multiply that number by 2.31 to get HEAD. Always get a pump with a HEAD rating at least double what you need.

Airstone

An airstone is also called an aquarium bubbler is a porous stone that is usually placed in an aquarium to diffuse air into the tank. Although an airstone is not necessary, it is recommended as it adds oxygen to the nutrient solution. Oxygen helps facilitate germination and healthy growth.

Types of Hydroponic Systems

Below are the most commonly used growing system for soilless gardening.

Wick System

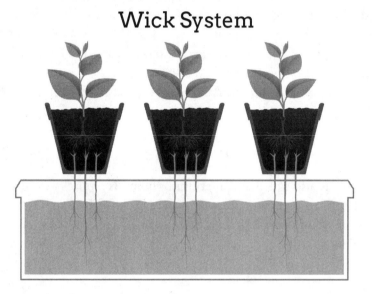

The wick system is a passive hydroponic system that has no moving parts. This makes it one of the easiest of all systems to operate. The nutrient solution is drawn up into the growing medium from a reservoir using a wick. This system can use a number of different growing medium such as perlite, vermiculite and coconut fibers. This type of system is best for lettuces, greens and herbs.

Caution: This system does not work well for large plants and the reservoir needs to be cleaned periodically.

Main parts:

- **Wick** - Fibrous rope, rayon rope, yarn, felt, nylon rope strips of fabric or old blankets make excellent wicks.

- **Grow tray** - The grow tray holds seeds or seedling and the growing medium.

- **Growing medium** - Choose a growing medium that absorbs water well. Good options are vermiculite, perlite or coconut coir. You can also use a soilless potting mix.

- **Reservoir** - The reservoir holds the water and nutrients. The bottom of the wick is suspended in the nutrient-enriched water. You don't need a complicated or fancy reservoir. However, a dark color is best to keep algae growth away. If you choose a clear container, it is best to paint it dark or create a shade covering. Be sure to keep the reservoir filled.

- **Aeration system (optional)** - An aeration system keeps oxygen levels in the water high which promotes healthy and quick growth. An aquarium pump or airstone and pump work well.

Deep Water Culture

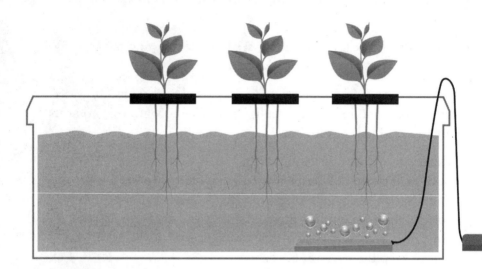

The water culture system is also fairly simple to operate. A platform, usually made of styrofoam, holds plants and this floats directly on the nutrient solution. Air is pumped to an airstone via a pump and this bubbles the nutrient solution and supplies oxygen to the roots of plants. This type of system is a great choice for growing leaf lettuce but not many other plants. This type of system can also easily be made out of an old aquarium or other watertight container.

Caution: This system requires quite a bit of water and electricity to operate.

Main Parts

- **Net pot** - This is a small round plastic basket with holes in it. The basket holds the plant and roots grow through the holes.

- **Reservoir** - Be sure to select a reservoir that will fit plants at full growth. Provide shade or paint your reservoir a dark color.

- **Lid/grow tray** - The lid or grow tray cradles the net pot so that it does not fall into the solution. You can also use a floating raft made from styrofoam.

- **Growing medium** - Rockwool cubes work well, as do packing peanuts, coconut fiber and expanded clay pellets.

- **Oxygen pump system** - Pump, tubing, airstone. The more bubbles the better. Bubbles need to make direct contact with the root systems to deliver oxygen. The water should appear like it is boiling. An aquarium air pump and airstone work really well and are easy to find at most pet stores.

Drip System

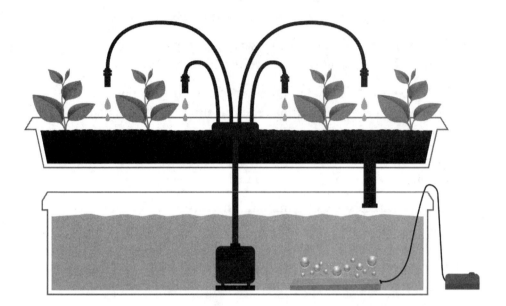

Drip systems are one of the most commonly used types of hydroponic systems today. The operation is pretty basic. A timer controls a submerged pump. The timer turns the pump on and plants receive nutrients via a small drip line. There are two types of drip systems, recovery and non-recovery. A recovery system collects excess nutrient solution that runs off and is collected back in the reservoir for re-use. This is the most commonly used home system Drip systems are great for larger plants such as cucumbers, tomatoes, peas, zucchini and even pumpkins.

Caution: pH needs to be checked periodically

Main Parts

- **Grow containers** - A popular choice is a 5-gallon bucket or several buckets connected together.

- **Reservoir** - The reservoir can sit at the side of the grow container and needs to hold enough nutrient enriched water to feed plants for a week.

- **Growing medium** - Some popular choices for this system include coco chips, perlite, vermiculite, clay pebbles and rockwool.

- **Tubing** - The size of your tubing should match your pump outlet and tube connectors.

- **Submersible pump** - Strong enough to deliver water from the reservoir to the grow containers but not so strong that it creates a fountain.

- **Timer** - Using a digital timer will allow you to set specific drip times each day. A 15 amp indoor/outdoor timer is ideal.

- **Drip stakes (optional)** - Drip stakes are plastic pegs that look like tent stakes. They attach to a drip line and carry the nutrient solution to the growing medium. They help the nutrients and water penetrate the medium faster resulting in less nutrient loss due to evaporation. Use two stakes per plant in case one gets clogged up. Keep an eye on them and soak them in a 10% vinegar solution to clean often.

Ebb-and-Flow System

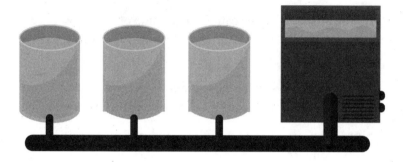

At first glance, an ebb-and-flow system looks complicated but in reality it is actually quite simple once set up. An ebb-and-flow system is pretty easy to manage and can be adapted for any size space.

In an ebb-and-flow system a submerged pump is connected to a timer and temporarily floods the grow tray with nutrient solution. When the pump turns off, the nutrient solution flows back into the reservoir. The timer is generally set to come of a few times each day, depending on the size of the system, type of plants, temperature and humidity and the growing medium used. This versatile system works with a number of growing mediums, including gravel or granular rockwool.

Caution: This system is vulnerable to power outages and pump failures.

Main Parts

Grow tray and reservoir - The grow tray and reservoir are connected in this type of system. The stacked container arrangement is most common for an ebb-and-flow system as it makes great use of space. One large container serves as the reservoir and a smaller container the same length and width serves as the grow tray. The grow tray fits on top of the reservoir and the empty space between will hold the nutrient water.

You can also place the grow tray on a separate table. Either way, the grow tray has to be above the reservoir for the pump to operate efficiently and create an ebb and flow. This type of design requires longer tubing and also requires more space.

There are two different grow tray layouts. The first is a single grow tray where all the plants are in one place with no separation. With this system, the entire tray is flooded at the same time with solution. The main benefit of this design is that it is easier to put together. However, plants can't be moved as easily.

The second type of grow tray uses individual containers for each plant. Containers are placed in tray that gets flooded with nutrient solution. You can grow a lot of plants in this system but the container can become heavy. Because of this, it is best to use the table set-up rather than the stacked container method for this system.

When planning the grow tray size it is important to think about the space that you have available as well as how many plants you wish to grow. The size of the reservoir is dependent on the space and how many plants you wish to water. Be sure that there is enough water to flood the grow tray. Smaller reservoirs require more frequent top-ups of nutrients. Growing plants will use water and nutrients more quickly. Keep in mind, it is always best to overestimate the size of the reservoir rather than underestimate it. Plants grow quickly.

Main Parts

- **Growing medium** - Grow trays can be filled with any type of growing medium with good choices being coconut fiber gravel, granulated rockwool, expanded clay pebbles and coconut fiber. Clay pebbles are the most popular choice if you place plants in the grow tray instead of individual containers. They hold plants in place well and need to be flooded every 2 hours. You can also use a combination of coconut fiber and perlite with two inches of clay pebbles on the bottom. This offers a secure foundation for young plants and prevents the medium from washing away when the tray is flooded.

- **Fill/drain overflow fitting kit** - You can find these kits at a garden store or online. They are inexpensive and are basically two hard plastic threaded pieces attached to a growing tray. There are different sizes available so be sure to get the correct size to match your tubing. The smallest piece if for the inlet and allows water to be pumped into the grow tray. The longer piece has slits that allow water to flow back to the reservoir.

- **Pump** - Strong enough to deliver water from the reservoir to the grow containers but not so strong that it creates a fountain.

- **Tubing** - Tubing size needs to match the fill/drain fitting and pump fitting. Clear tubing is the best.

- **Timer** - Using a digital timer will allow you to set specific flood times each day. A 15 amp indoor/outdoor timer is ideal.

Nutrient Film (N.F.T.)

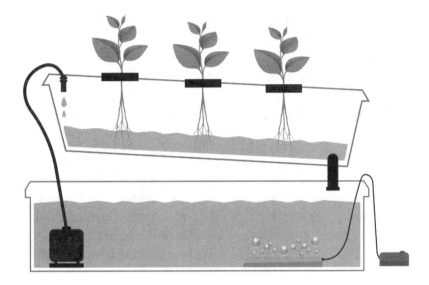

N.F.T. systems are what most people think of when they think hydroponics. These systems have a constant flow of nutrients solution with no timer. This system works with gravity to send a thin film of nutrient solution over the exposed roots. One of the major benefits of this type of system is that plants receive a constant flow of nutrients.

A pump circulates the solution into the growing tray or channel and it flows over the plant roots and drains back into a reservoir. There is no growing medium used apart from air, which saves money. Plants are supported by a small plastic basket with the roots hanging in the nutrient solution. This system does not require an extensive setup or constant monitoring like other systems. The only real upkeep is a weekly change of the nutrient solution.

The slope of the channel determines how fast the water will flow through the system. A recommended slope is a 1:30 or 1:40 ratio.

What this means is that you want a one inch drop for each 30 to 40 inches of horizontal length. With quick-growing plants such as herbs and lettuce, a flow rate of 0.5 to 1 liter per minute is recommended. The best thing to do is to set the system up to adjust if needed. Be sure that your channel is as straight as possible.

N.F.T. is great for small plants like lettuces and herbs.

Caution: Plants are vulnerable to water shortages due to power outages.

Main Parts

- **Reservoir -** The size or your reservoir is dependent on the size of your system. If your reservoir is too small it will cause instability in the nutrient solution. Be sure to choose the correct size. Place the reservoir below the channels to ensure that the pump works properly.

- **Grow tubes -** Food-grade plastic pipe, stainless steel and rain gutters are common grow tubes or channels. Channels should be big enough to accomodate the root system of mature plants. For instance, strawberries need about six inches and tomatoes need about eight inches. The channel must be covered to prevent the sun from contacting the plant's roots.

- **Growing baskets -** Set grow baskets in holes cut in the cover of the channel. Remember that baskets should not touch the water. Roots should dangle in the air allowing just the tips to touch the solution. Starter cubes work really well with this type of system and you can use a little growing medium if necessary.

- **Submersible pump -** Strong enough to deliver water from the reservoir to the grow containers but not so strong that it creates a fountain.

- **Tubing -** The size of your tubing should match your pump outlet and tube connectors.

Aeroponics

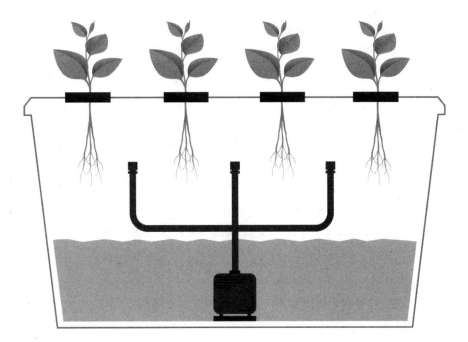

Aeroponic systems are the most high-tech type of hydroponic gardening. Similar to N.F.T. systems, aeroponics the growing medium is mostly air. Plant roots hang in the air and are misted with nutrient solutions. Misting generally happens every few minutes. Also like N.F.T. systems, roots dry out quickly if the misting cycle is interrupted. A timer controls the pump that delivers the mist.

Caution: This is an expensive system to operate, sprinkler heads can clog and plants are vulnerable to water shortages due to power outages.

Main Parts

- **Enclosed grow chamber** - This chamber must be airtight and opaque so that no light gets in. A large opaque tote bin works well. Be sure that it is tall enough for your roots to hang down and not touch the bottom.

- **Net pots** - To hold the plants.

- **Misting/sprinkler heads** - Misting heads can be purchased online or at garden stores. There are many types to choose from. Be sure to do your homework before purchasing. You want the misting heads to overlaps so that all roots will be covered by the spray.

- **Submersible pump** - Strong enough to deliver water from the reservoir to the grow containers but not so strong that it creates a fountain.

- **Reservoir** - In the simplest setups the grow chamber and the reservoir are the same size but it may vary depending on the exact setup.

- **Tubing** - The size of your tubing should match your pump outlet and tube connectors.

- **Timer** - Using a digital timer will allow you to set specific mist times each day. A 15 amp indoor/outdoor timer is ideal.

Kratky Method

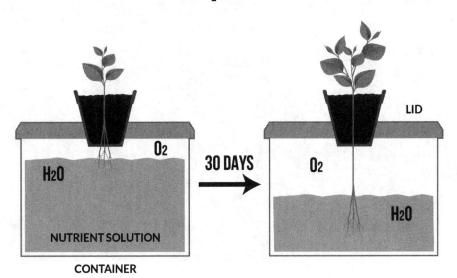

The Kratky method is a simple passive growing technique that requires no pumps or electricity for the growth cycle. This method is similar to a standard hydroponic deep water culture or raft system apart from the fact that the raft sits fixed atop a reservoir filled with water and nutrient solution and which stays stagnant. As the growth cycle progresses, the water levels drops as roots grow which creates an "air zone" for the roots.

When the plant is ready for harvest, the nutrient solution is almost gone. To grow a new crop you simply just replenish water and nutrient solution and put fresh transplants on the top of the tank. Because you determine the amount of nutrient solution needed only once for each grow, there is no additional adjustments necessary. This is a great system for people who want to keep growing as simple as possible. The best plants to grow with this system are lettuces and herbs.

Caution: The reservoir must be thoroughly cleaned at least once every three to five growing cycles.

"It takes half your life before you discover life is a do-it-yourself project."

— **Napoleon Hill** (1883 - 1970)

SIMPLE HERB HYDROPONIC KRATKY PROJECT

One of the most fun parts of growing hydroponically is creating your own system to grow a plentiful harvest. This simple passive Kratky system is great for leafy greens and herbs.

Supplies

- 4 wide mouth mason jars, clean
- Black spray paint
- 4 x 3.5" net grow pots/baskets
- Nutrients
- 2 cups expanded clay pebbles
- 4 herb transplants

How to make it

1   Paint jars black and let dry

2   Fill jars ¾ full with water

3   Add nutrients

4   Add net pots

5   Add a thin layer of pebbles in the baskets

6   Carefully rinse and pull apart roots on transplants

7   Set herbs in grow pots

8   Add more pebbles to hold plants in place

9   Place jars in an area where they will get bright light

10 Top up water as needed

11 Change out nutrient solution weekly

12 Harvest herbs regularly

Optional: You can start seeds in rockwool cubes if desired.

MORE EASY PROJECTS

Here are more hydroponic systems that you can easily make at home.

Wicking Soda Bottle System

If you want a really super simple project to do with your kids, this is it.

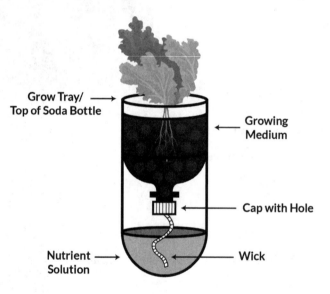

Grow Tray/
Top of Soda Bottle

Growing
Medium

Cap with Hole

Nutrient
Solution

Wick

Supplies

- 1 plastic 2-liter soda bottle, cleaned, with cap

- Clean and sharp scissors

- Duct tape

- Plastic black spray paint

- Wicking material

- Growing medium

- Nutrient solution

- Plants

Making it

1 Cut the bottle 8" from the top

2 Cover the cut edges with duct tape

3 Spray paint the bottom portion of the bottle with black paint and let it it dry

4 Cut a hole in the cap large enough to thread the wicking material through

5 Thread wicking material through the hole so that you have half of the material on each side of the hole

6 Combine the nutrient solution and water per instructions

7 Fill the base of the soda bottle to 4 inches from the top

8 Invert the top of the bottle and fill it with growing medium. Make sure that the wick is weaved and stretched through the medium

9 Plant your seedlings in the growing medium

10 Place the bottle top cap-side down into the bottle half of the bottle. Be sure that the wick rests freely in the nutrient solution

11 Make sure that the bottle cap is above the water level and the wick is hanging into the nutrients.

Tips for caring for your system:

- When water and nutrient solution gets low, replace it with a new mixture.

- Flush the growing medium with clean and fresh water every two weeks to prevent harmful nutrient buildup.

Aquarium Water Culture System

This is a great project if you have an old aquarium hanging around. If you don't, you can always find them at yard sales.

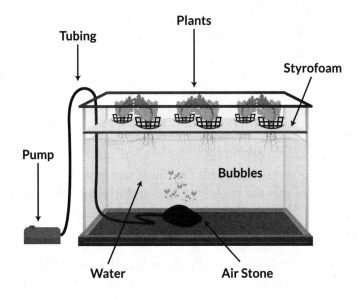

Supplies

- An airtight glass aquarium

- Material for a light shield — aluminum or cardboard

- 2 inch thick piece of styrofoam for raft, cut to fit loosely inside reservoir

- Net pots to hold plants

- Growing medium, best is clay pebbles

- Aeration system: air pup, airstone and tubing

- Nutrients

- pH test kit

- Sharp knife

- Plants

STEP 1
Cut Holes In Styrofoam

STEP 2
Add Growing Medium

STEP 3
Fill Reservoir With Water

Aquarium

Making it

1 Cut holes in the styrofoam to fit your net pots. The bottom of the pots should hang just below the styrofoam

2 Add growing medium to each pot

3 Fill aquarium with water

4 Mix nutrients per instructions and add to water

5 Test the pH and adjust. Keep in mind that different plants require different pH levels

6 Attach tubing to airstone and place in water

7 Attach other end of tubing to the pump and place outside of the aquarium

8 Plug in teh pup to be sure that air stone is producing bubbles

9 Place the styrofoam platform on top of the water

10 Put seedlings in net cups

11 Place in each pot in a hole in the platform. Check to be sure that the plant's roos are submerged but not the stem

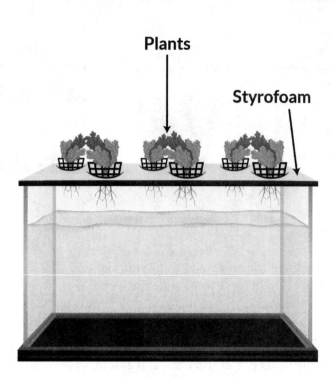

Plants

Styrofoam

Tips for caring for your system:

- Add water only when plants have absorbed half of the nutrients.

- Check pH and adjust only if needed.

- The second time that the plants have absorbed the solution refresh the nutrients by draining the reservoir completely and making a fresh batch

Five Gallon Bucket Deep Water Culture System

This system uses a clean 5 gallon bucket with a lid.

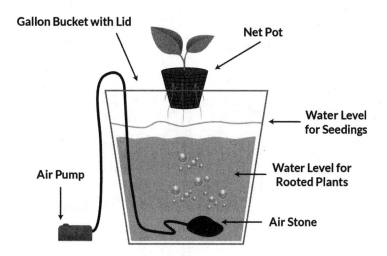

Supplies

- 5 gallon bucket with lid
- Net pot
- Aeration system: air pump, airstone and tubing
- Growing medium
- Nutrients
- pH test kit
- Plants

Making it

1   Follow instructions for the aquarium system. The only variation is that instead of cutting a hole for the net pot in styrofoam, you cut a hole in the lid of the bucket. Be sure to make the hole smaller than the pot so it does not slip through.

Five Gallon Bucket Aeroponic System

This system uses a five gallon bucket with a lid and is fairly simple to construct. Because this project uses a pump and a timer, you will need to position it near an electrical outlet.

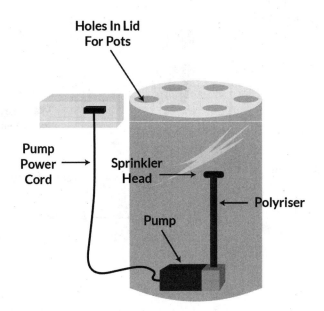

Supplies

- 5 gallon clean bucket with lid
- Net pots
- Timer
- Pump
- Hole saw
- Drill

- 1 360 degree sprinkler head with ½" thread
- ½ inch by 1/2 inch threaded poly riser
- Regular saw
- Plants
- Clay pebbles (if needed)

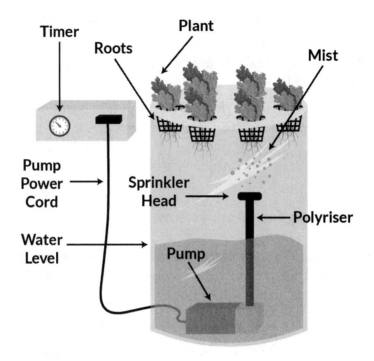

Timer | Roots | Plant | Mist

Pump
Power → Sprinkler
Cord | Head | → Polyriser

Water
Level | → Pump

Making it

1   Cut holes in the bucket of the lid to fit your net pots. Be sure to space them evenly and make sure that they fit snugly and won't fall through the holes

2   Screw the threaded poly riser into the pup. Cut it to the desired height

3   Attach the sprinkler head to the top of the poly riser. Be sure that the height of both the riser and sprinkler head are lower than the expected length of the roots

4   Put the pump with the attached riser and sprinkler head into the bucket

5   Thread the pump cord through one of the holes in the lid and attach to the timer

6   Put two gallons of water into the bucket along with nutrient solution per directions

7   Place the lid on top of the bucket and arrange plants in pots. Use clay pebbles to keep them in place if necessary

8   Turn on pump

Tips for caring for your system:

- Pay very close attention to the temperature of your grow space. Because the roots are exposed it is easy for them to get too hot. Grow lights can make matters worse

- The reservoir temperature should be kept at 64F or just below

- Clean filters, pumps and turning regularly to avoid clogs

- Because this system works to grow plants quickly, it is imperative to keep a close eye on operations

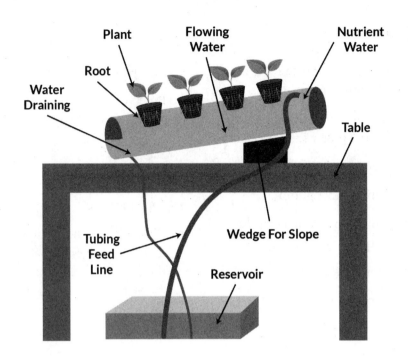

Plant
Flowing Water
Nutrient Water
Root
Water Draining
Table
Tubing Feed Line
Wedge For Slope
Reservoir

PVC Nutrient Film Technique System

Putting the pre-planning into this project will help you have great success. You can hang the system from the ceiling, prop it up on wooden stands or place it on a table with a built-in slope. Remember, this system is gravity driven so the most important thing to remember is flow. With that in mind, one end of the channel must be higher than the other but not too high. For this project, aim for 1 inch of slope per 20 to 40 inches of horizontal length. Before building, decide where you want to place this system and what plants you are growing. You can make this system as simple as placing it on a table and propping up one end with wedges. Be sure to place this system close to an electrical outlet.

Supplies

- 4 inch food grade PVC pipe, 30 inches long

- 2 adjustable rubber end caps for the pipe with hose clamps

- Net pots

- Submersible pump

- Irrigation tubing to fit the output of your pump

- Plumbers cement

- Growing medium

- Nutrients

- Reservoir container with lid (20 gallons or bigger)

- Drill

- Hole saw

- Tape measure

- Zip ties, wire shelf hangers, luber, or wedges to make slope

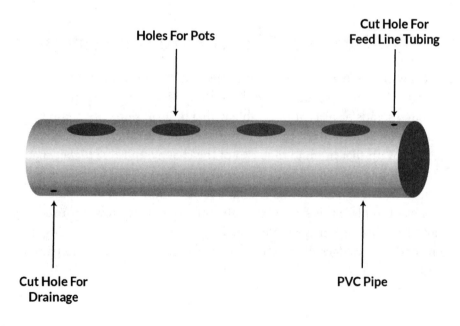

Holes For Pots

Cut Hole For Feed Line Tubing

Cut Hole For Drainage

PVC Pipe

Making it

1   Cut holes in the top of the tipe for your net pots. Keep pots about 3 inches apart to allow room for growth. Make sure that cups just sit in holes and don't fall through

2   Place the rubber caps on the ends of the pipe

3   Cut another hole in the top of the pipe for your tubing that will carry the nutrients from the reservoir. Make the hole the correct size so that the tubing fits snugly

4   On the opposite end of the pipe, cut a hole in the bottom to fit tubing. This will drain water to the reservoir. Place the hole beyond where the roots sit as you don't want it to drain until it reaches the very last plant

5   Determine the ideal slope for the system

6   Use wire or zip ties to attach pipe to the ceiling in a room ro build a wooden stand for your system. You can also place on a table and use little wedges to create a slope

7   Cut two holes in the lid of the reservoir for the irrigation tubing. One for output and one for input

8   Place the water pump in the bottom of the reservoir

9   Attach the irrigation host to the pump and use plumbers cement to secure the seal

10   Feed the irrigation hose to your reservoir lid and to the hole in the pipe

11   Connect another length of tubing form the hole in the bottom of the pipe to the second hole in the lid. Secure with plumber's cement

12   Fill reservoir with water and nutrients per directions

13   Fill growing pots with medium and plants and put them in holes in pipe

14   Turn on the pump and test system for leaks and slope. The roots should touch the flowing water

Tips for caring for your system:

- Check pH often and adjust as needed
- Keep an eye on the pump to be sure that it is functioning properly
- Keep an eye on roots and be sure that they don't block the growing channel
- Inspect tubing for blockages
- Change out nutrient solution weekly

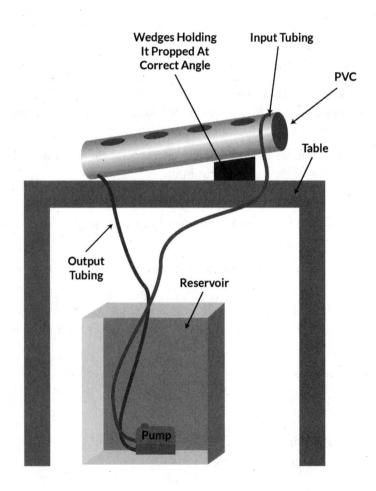

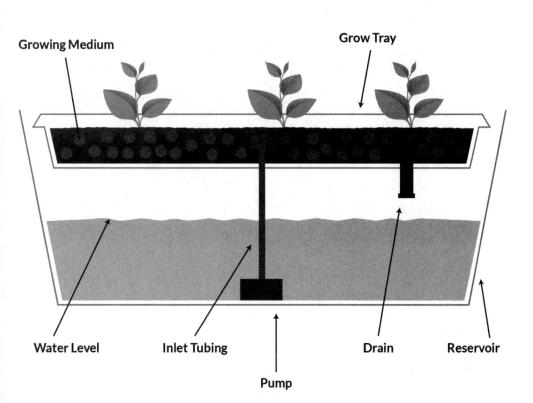

Growing Medium

Grow Tray

Water Level

Inlet Tubing

Drain

Reservoir

Pump

Plastic Storage Stacked Container Ebb-and-Flow System

You will need access to an electrical outlet for this system and keep lighting in mind. A level surface is necessary so that water anc drain efficiently and plant will get plenty of oxygen.

Supplies

- 16-20 gallon storage tote, opaque or dark colored
- 30 quart clear storage tote, or a size that will fit snugly on top of the larger tote
- Timer
- Clay pebbles or other medium
- Grow containers
- Drill
- Irrigation tubing, ½ inch diameter, 18 inches long
- Submersible pump with ½ inch fittings
- Wooden dowel longer than the height of the tallest container
- Nutrients
- Plants

Making it

1   Drill two holes in the bottom of the small container. An inlet hole for water going into the grow tray and an outlet hole for water draining out. The inlet hole needs to accommodate the fill fitting. The outlet hole is where the tubing goes so e sure it is a little smaller than tubing

2   Attach the fill fitting set to the inlet hole

3   Cut a piece of hose that will connect the inlet fitting to the pump outlet. Be sure that the length is long enough for the pump to sit at the bottom of the reservoir while the grow tray is on top. You might have to adjust it several times to get it right. Be sure that the fit is secure on both ends

4   Place the pump at the bottom of the reservoir

5   Cut a piece of hose for the overflow. It should be long enough to be above the anticipated water flood height in the grow tray and still reach the reservoir without touching the water. Fit the tubing into the overflow hole and attach the overflow fitting to the top of the tubing so it is in the grow tray

6   Run the pump cord between the two containers so that the plug is on the outside of the system

7   FIll the reservoir with 2 gallons of water at a time. After each addition, measure the increase in water level with a wooden dowel, marking each increment. This will allow you to know how much nutrient-water your plants are using and how much you need to add

8   Fill to a total of 10 gallons of water

9   Add the nutrients per instructions

10   Fill plant containers with medium

11   Plant seedlings in containers, arranging the growing medium to keep them in place

12   Place containers in grow tray and fit the tray on top of the reservoir. Keep pump plug cord out

13   Set the timer and pump to flood three times a day for 15 minutes per cycle

Tips for caring for your system:

- Water new plants in your system from the top daily for a few days until they are used to the system

- Inspect the system daily to be sure that the drain is working properly

- Change the nutrient water weekly

THE GROWING PROCESS

First and foremost it is important to remember the basics of growing any plant hydroponically:

- Know the temperature that your plant requires for optimal growth and keep that as constant as you can

- Keep a moderate level of humidity

- Choose and use the best source of lighting for your plants

- Provide plenty of fresh air for adequate levels of $Co2$

- Provide oxygen to roots with a pump or agitation

- Keep the pH where it needs to be

- Keep the nutrient solution concentration consistent

It is always best to do research specific to the plants that you will be growing before starting a hydroponic project.

Starting Seeds

Starting seeds is a great way to baby your plants through the entire growing process. Keep in mind, some plants do better from seeds while others do best from transplants. To start from seeds you will need an area with high humidity and a growing media.

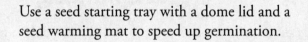

Use a seed starting tray with a dome lid and a seed warming mat to speed up germination.

Starting mediums: You can use a number of materials for a starting medium including sponges, coconut fiber or perlite produce.

1   Moisten the starting medium using half-strength nutrient solution

2   Be sure that the starting medium is between 72 and 80 degrees Fahrenheit and the surrounding air temperature is about the same

3   At first, before the seeds have sprouted, expose the tray to soft light

4   Once you see sprouts, move to brighter light

5   Be sure to keep the medium moderately moist using half strength solution through the initial stages

Transplanting

You can move your plants over to your hydroponic system once you see a noticeable root system. This is easiest if you are using sponges but if you are using a looser starter medium use basket liners to make things easier. Embed your seedlings well into the planting medium and user low light to start, increasing in three to four days

TIPS FOR SUCCESS

As with any new venture, growing a successful hydroponic garden requires some attention to detail and commitment. Maintaining your system, no matter how simple, will ensure a bountiful harvest of fresh and nutritious food. Here are some things to keep in mind.

- **Cleanliness** - Starting off with clean equipment is essential to success. Clean grow trays, pots boxes and reservoirs with a 10% bleach solution. As your plants start to grow, be sure to remove any fallen debris, including leaves, as this will keep bacteria at bay.

- **Nutrient solution** - For best results, change out your nutrient solution weekly or at minimum, top off your system with clean water.

- **Watering** - Watering frequency is totally dependent on what type of system you are using. However, a general rule of thumb would be to water enough that roots stay wet but not saturated. If you see that the growing medium and the roots are getting dry between watering cycles you need to increase the irrigation frequency. If they are wet all the time, decrease the frequency. Keep in mind that as plants grow their water needs will change. Plants don't need water at night and will absorb the majority of water when it is light. If using a timer, plan on running irrigation cycles during the day but if you notice that they are drying out at night you can add an irrigation cycle at night. Watering is one of those things that will become second nature once you get the hang of it.

- **Reservoir temperature** - The temperature in the reservoir should be around 70 F. If it is hard for you to keep this temperature you can consider a heating mat below the reservoir. A small aquarium heater will work for smaller units. If the temperature is too hot, add clean ice packs. You can also wrap your reservoir in foil to reduce temperature. If necessary, install a water chiller.

- **Humidity** - The first thing to remember is that temperature and humidity are not the same. Different plants require different humidity levels; be sure that you know what your plants need. In addition, plants require different humidity levels at various stages of growth. At the seedling stage, plants require high humidity, above 80%. This encourages germination. Most plants are happy with humidity levels between 55% and 65% after germination. Too much humidity can create a breeding ground for pests while too little can cause plants to dry out. Purchase a hygrometer for your grow space to ensure adequate humidity. If you need to add humidity, a humidifier is a great option. However, simply misting the air a few times a day can also have a positive impact on humidity. If you need to decrease humidity consider ventilating the grow space. Fresh air can do wonders! If this doesn't do the trick you may need to add a dehumidifier or a fan.

- **Equipment** - Depending on your system, a hydroponic garden can have a lot of moving parts. Any one of these parts can fail at any time and this could end in catastrophe for your garden. Keep a regular check on all parts and keep replacements on hand for a quick and easy fix.

- **Watch your plants** - A daily inspection of not only your system but also your plants will help you spot irregularities before it is too late. Look at the roots, leaves, stalks and keep and eye on the overall health of your plants.

- **Keep a growing journal** - The best success comes only after making and correcting mistakes. Taking notes will help you have the biggest and best plants ever. Make notes on solutions, equipment, maintenance, etc. Taking consistent and thorough notes will be useful for improving your technique and results.

- **Change only one thing at a time** - If you make too many changes at a time it can be very difficult to know what is and isn't working. Make one change and allow some time for observation. Keep notes and change something else if necessary.

- **Start with healthy plants** - Whether you grow your own plants from seeds or purchase transplants for your system, always be sure that they are healthy and robust. Remember also that you don't need soil for hydroponic growing so be sure to rinse the soil gently from the roots before placing a plant into a hydroponic grow basket.

OVERCOMING OBSTACLES

Although the challenges with hydroponic gardening are different than conventional gardening, some similar issues can occur that are mostly related to environmental conditions. Knowing what to watch for a how to respond will help keep your garden operating efficiently.

Diseases

In conventional gardening, fungus and bacteria thrive in the soil. In hydroponic growing the most common causes of disease are environmental in nature. Disease can spread rapidly in close growing conditions so it is important that plants have enough individual growing space and that you remove infected plants when necessary. Using root stimulators in the early growth stages can help keep disease at bay as well. Other ways to ensure healthy plants are to monitor solutions and pH carefully.

Here are a few diseases that you may have to combat.

- **Root rot -** This condition is the result of too much water or pathogens in the growing medium. Plants will turn yellow and wilt. Roots may turn mushy. To avoid root rot, keep the moisture levels in your system balanced and follow tips for success as noted above.

- **Powdery mildew -** This fungal infection appears like baby powder sprinkled on leaves. Leaves become yellow and fall off if not remedied. Too much humidity can cause powdery mildew, so keep an eye on levels and reduce if needed.

- **Gray mold -** This mold begins with small spots on leaves that turn gray and fuzzy and cause the plant to turn brown and mushy. This condition is common in overly humid areas.

- **Downy mildew -** Like powdery mildew, downy mildew causes white markings on the leave which eventually turn yellow. Found on the underside of leaves, downy mildew occurs in overly wet weather or when leaves have been wet for too long.

Pests

Although the potential for a pest problem is not as great in soilless gardening as in conventional methods, it is not an impossibility. The big issue with pests in a hydroponic system is that the system is interconnected and if a problem is not noticed it can quickly get out of hand. Therefore, it is imperative that you remain diligent and know what to look for. Here are some pest that could become an issue.

- **Aphids** - Aphids, often called plant lice, are small and can be green, black or grey in color. They are often found around plant stems and suck the juices out of leaves, turning them yellow.

- **Thrips** - Thrips are parasitic insects that are extremely hard to see because they are so tiny. However, as tiny as they are, they can cause massive destruction. If thrips are a problem you will see very small metallic black spots on the tips of the leaves. After this, leaves turn yellow, then brown and dry out.

- **Fungus gnats** - This pest causes great damage at the larvae stage when larvae feed on plant roots This can cause infections, stunt growth and can even kill the plant.

- **White flies** - White flies look a lot like white moths and are quick to fly away when a plant is disturbed making them very hard to catch. They cause white spots and yellowing on plants.

- **Spider mites** - Like other pests, spider mites are tiny and very had to notice until after you see the damage they have done. To check plants for spider mites it is best to look for a spider-type webbing around the leaves and stem. You can also gently wipe the underside of the leaves with a soft tissue to check for spider mite blood.

Combating Pests

Although a well-kept hydroponic garden has very few problems with pests, here are some tips just in case.

- **Sticky traps** - Place a few sticky traps in the room where you have your system and some at the base of your plants. Yellow traps work well for fungus gnats and white flies, while blue traps work for thrips.

- **Beneficial predators** - Placing beneficial predators such as nematodes in the growing medium also will reduce pests.

- **Horticultural oils and herbal extracts** - There are a number of effective organic oils and extracts that do a great job controlling pests such as spider mites and aphids. These include rosemary, cinnamon, garlic, cloves, neem and soybean oil.

Nutrient Deficiencies

Nutrient deficiency can occur when plants use nutrient solution quicker than it is replaced. It is imperative to keep an eye on plants and adjust how often you are changing the solution or adding nutrients. You can also supplement with the missing nutrient, although this can be a bit hit and miss.

Here are some signs of nutrient deficiency to watch for:

- **Nitrogen** - Growth may be stunted, lower leaves yellow or the entire plant may be light green in color

- **Phosphorus** - Plants that are lacking in this nutrients turn blue-green in color and have stunted growth

- **Potassium** - Dead spots appear on leaf edges and leaves seem papery in appearance. Overall growth is also stunted

- **Magnesium** - Bottom leaves become wilted and yellow around the edges.

- **Calcium** - Leaves, stems and new growth dies

- **Zinc** - Spaces between the veins in leaves are yellowish in color and have a papery thin appearance

- **Iron** - The veins in plants lacking iron are very green but the rest of the leaf turns yellow

- **Copper** - The edges of leaves curl and become blue or dark green in color

- **Sulfur** - Growth is stunted and old leaves remain green while new ones turn yellow

- **Manganese** - Growth is stunted and bottom leaves become checkered yellow and green

- **Molybdenum** - Leaves are stunted, malformed and yellow

- **Boron** - Tips of leaves are scorched in appearance

Algae Bloom

If you see a little stain or slimy film on the surface of your nutrient solution, it may be algae bloom. Algae are very small aquatic plant organisms that can be green, black, red or brown. It can smell like mold or dirt. The big issue with algae is that it gobbles up nutrients and oxygen while blocking hoses and pumps. Algae can also attract fungus and gnats which will eat plant roots.

Since algae are plants they like the same condition that plants like — light, nutrients, warmth and moisture. Of these, light is really the only one that you can alter. Because of this, the best way to control algae is to take a preventative approach. Use a reservoir that is dark colored or spray paint a clear one dark.

Algae also can bloom on top of your growing medium. The best thing to do is to wash the growing medium carefully with clean water. This can sometimes be difficult to do and you may have to wait until after harvest to clean everything well. Keeping all your equipment clean will help combat algae.

TOP 11 HYDROPONIC
FRUITS & VEGETABLES

Lettuce

Favorable temp: cool. pH: 6.0 - 7.0

If you are new to hydroponics, lettuces are the perfect place to start. They grow fast in a hydroponic system and are easy to take care of. You can grow lettuce in any type of system but the simplest is a water culture system or a wick system.

Spinaches

Favorable temp: cool to warm. pH: 6.0 - 7.0

Spinach is a cool plant that does not require much light. Harvest all at once or just tear a few leaves off at a time. You can get about 12 weeks of continuous harvesting in good conditions. Like lettuce, spinach can be grown in any system but does well in a simple water culture or wick system.

Kale

Favorable temp: cool to warm. pH: 5.5 - 6.5

Kale is a super healthy green that is very much at home in a hydroponic water system. Like spinach and lettuce it is happy in a water culture system. Kale grows quickly. Just six weeks from transplant to harvest and can be partially harvested for a continual supply.

Beans

Favorable temp: warm. pH: 6.0

Beans are considered one of the most productive and low-maintenance veggies that can be grown hydroponically. The best thing is that you can choose from any type of bean, including green beans, pole beans, lima beans and pinto beans. Be sure to have a trellis handy to support bean plants. You can harvest after six to eight weeks and a crop will last from three to four months. Beans do best in an ebb-and-flow system with a heavy medium such as clay pellets or gravel.

Tomatoes

Favorable temp: hot. pH: 5.5 - 6.5

If you plan to grow tomatoes indoors be sure to purchase a good grow light system as tomatoes require a great deal of light. A number of types of tomatoes can be grown but the most popular in home hydroponic systems is cherry tomatoes. Tomatoes are hardy plants that can can thrive in most any hydroponic system. However, there are three in which tomatoes really excel:, nutrient film, ebb-and-flow and drip systems.

Strawberries

Favorable temp: warm. pH: 6.0

Strawberries are one of the most popular plants grown in commercial hydroponic productions. Large-scale nutrient film technique systems often are used for mass production. Growing strawberries in a home hydroponic system is a rewarding and delicious experience. Because strawberries have a small root system, they grow well in a hydroponic system. Simple systems or more complex systems work for growing strawberries in a hydroponic fashion. You can use deep water culture, ebb-andflow, nutrient film technique, drip irrigation, wick system or aeroponics. Deep-water culture accommodates a large number of plants in a single tiered system. Day-neutral types of strawberries are the best for all year production because they are not impacted by changes in light or temperature.

Blueberries

Favorable temp: warm. pH: 4.5 - 6.0

Although blueberries will not bear fruit until the second year, it is well worth the wait. Since blueberries are hard to plant from seeds, transplants are best. A nutrient film technique system will produce the best results. Blueberries are better suited for more advanced hydroponic gardeners than novices.

Cucumbers

Favorable temp: hot. pH: 5.5 - 6.0

If you like cucumbers you will get a hefty harvest growing them hydroponically. Like tomatoes, cucumbers are a warm temperature plant and need plenty of light and warm temperatures to do well. Several types of cucumbers are well-suited to soilless growing, including American slicers, long thin-skinned European and smooth-skinned Lebanese cucumbers. Rockwool starter cubes are the best way to grow hydroponic cucumbers.

Radishes

Favorable temp: cool. pH: 6.0 - 7.0

You can't really go wrong growing radishes in soil or without soil. They are a very rewarding crop and make an excellent beginner hydroponic project. Because radishes do well in cool temperatures they do not need any additional grow lights.

Peppers

Favorable temp: warm to hot. pH: 5.5 - 6.0

Peppers are similar to tomatoes as far as the kind of growing conditions they prefer. They like warm temperature and plenty of light. They often take about three months to mature. You can start seeds or get small plants from a garden shop. The best kinds to grow hydroponically include jalapeño and habanero for hot and mazurka, cubico, nairobi, and fellini for sweet peppers.

Chives

Favorable temp: warm to hot. pH: 6.0

It is easiest to grow chives from a plant in a hydroponic system. It take six to eight weeks for chives to fully mature and you can harvest them regularly. Chives require a lot of light for 12 to 14 hours each day.

Basil

Favorable temp: warm. pH: 5.5 - 6.5

Basil does very well in a hydroponic system and does really well in a
N.F.T. or a drip system. When the plant matures, you can harvest and
trim weekly. Provide plenty of light, at least 11 hours daily.

Mints

Favorable temp: warm. pH: 5.5 - 6.5

Mints, including peppermint and spearmint, have been grown extensively in hydroponics systems. One of the main advantages of growing mint hydroponically is that it contains the roots. When grown conventionally, mint can take over a garden space quickly.

"The love of gardening is a seed once sown that never dies."

— Gertrude Jekyll

GETTING FISHY: AQUAPONICS

At its simplest, aquaponics is raising fish (aquaculture) and growing food together hydroponically in a mutually beneficial environment. The waste from the fish provides an organic food source for plants while the plants naturally filter the water for the fish. Microbes convert ammonia from fish waste into nitrites, and then into nitrates. Nitrates are a form of oxygen that plants uptake and use to grow. Solid fish waste becomes vermicompost that also feeds plants.

A Brief History

The term aquaponics was coined during the Cold War-era America, when the fear of an A-bomb resulted in combining fish farming and soilless gardening. Research revealed that this type of growing system could produce nutritious food successfully in a symbiotic system in a very small space.

However, aquaponics has roots way back in time. The ancient Chinese used a similar process whereby fish helped control insects in rice paddies and provided fertilizer to plants. A similar form of agriculture whereby plants grow on floating structures and rely on the nutrients provided by aquatic life has been used by a number of other ancient cultures, including the Aztecs in Mexico and the Uru people in Bolivia as well as the Egyptians of the Nile Delta.

A Very Simple System

Although some people shy away from aquaponics, thinking that it is way too complicated, it is actually quite simple not only to set up but also to operate. Look at it this way, if you have weeds or plants in your aquarium, you are practicing aquaponics.

As mentioned above, the system contains three parts:

- Fish
- Plants
- Bacteria

These three parts live together in a mutually beneficial environment. Achieving a correct balance of each ensures the environment will be healthy for all.

The beginning of the aquaponics system starts when fish are fed, they excrete waste. The majority of this waste is ammonia, which can kill fish at high levels. Enter the nitrifying bacteria that break it down into useable plant food. Plants absorb the food and send filtered water back to the fish tank.

Hydroponics vs. Aquaponics vs. Traditional Gardening

While there are definite similarities between hydroponics and aquaponics, there are significant differences. The main focus in hydroponic gardening is that no soil is used and the main focus in aquaponics gardening is on the relationship between plants and fish. Both systems are indeed different from conventional gardening:

Garden Type	Light	Water	Nutrients
Traditional	Sun	Rain/Irrigation	Soil/Amendments
Hydroponic	Sun/Artificial	Cycled	Custom Mixes
Aquaponic	Artificial	Cycled	From Fish

Big Benefits of Aquaponics

Many people start out with hydroponics, get the hang of soilless growing and move on to raise fish as well. The big benefits of aquaponics are that you can raise food organically and also raise fish to eat at the same time. This gives you basically two crops in one! The fish generally used in an aquaponic system are carp and trout, which have high levels of healthy omega-3 fatty acids. Of course, you don't have to raise the fish to eat. They can just be an interesting and integral part of your system for raising plants. The most humble of all fish, the goldfish, is king among all others when it comes to a small aquaponics system.

Ready to take your hydroponic garden to the next level?
Consider aquaponics!